MATH ON THE JOB

Building a Business

This could be you!

Rick Wunderlich

Crabtree Publishing Company

www.crabtreebooks.com

Crabtree Publishing Company
www.crabtreebooks.com

Dedicated by Rick Wunderlich
To my Jesse, who loves family first and business second.

Author: Rick Wunderlich

Editorial director: Kathy Middleton

Editors: Reagan Miller, Janine Deschenes, and
 Kathy Middleton

Proofreader: Crystal Sikkens

Photo research: Margaret Amy Salter

Designer: Margaret Amy Salter

Production coordinator and prepress technician:
 Margaret Amy Salter

Print coordinator: Katherine Berti

Math consultant: Diane Dakers

Special thanks to Josh and Holly Allen,
Owners of Dee-O-Gee, Bozeman, MT

Photographs:
Shutterstock: © Radu Bercan: p9; © Lauren Elisabeth: p29;

All other images by Shutterstock

Library and Archives Canada Cataloguing in Publication

Wunderlich, Rick, author
  Math on the job : building a business / Richard Wunderlich.

(Math on the job)
Includes index.
Issued in print and electronic formats.
ISBN 978-0-7787-2357-8 (bound).--
ISBN 978-0-7787-2363-9 (paperback).--
ISBN 978-1-4271-1738-0 (html)

  1. Business mathematics--Juvenile literature. 2. Mathematics--
Juvenile literature. I. Title. II. Title: Building a business.

HF5691.W96 2016   j510   C2015-908037-1
                                         C2015-908038-X

Library of Congress Cataloging-in-Publication Data

Names: Wunderlich, Richard, author.
Title: Math on the job. Building a business / Richard Wunderlich.
Other titles: Building a business
Description: Series: Math on the job | Includes index. | Description
    based on print version record and CIP data provided by publisher;
    resource not viewed.
Identifiers: LCCN 2015046627 (print) | LCCN 2015045154 (ebook) |
    ISBN 9781427117380 (electronic HTML) |
    ISBN 9780778723578 (reinforced library binding : alk. paper) |
    ISBN 9780778723639 (pbk. : alk. paper)
Subjects: LCSH: Mathematics--Juvenile literature. | Business
    mathematics--Juvenile literature.
Classification: LCC HF5691 (print) | LCC HF5691 .W88 2016 (ebook)
    | DDC 510--dc23
LC record available at http://lccn.loc.gov/2015046627

Crabtree Publishing Company
www.crabtreebooks.com   1-800-387-7650

Printed in Canada/022016/IH20151223

Published in Canada
Crabtree Publishing
616 Welland Ave.
St. Catharines, ON
L2M 5V6

Published in the United States
Crabtree Publishing
PMB 59051
350 Fifth Avenue, 59th Floor
New York, New York 10118

Published in the United Kingdom
Crabtree Publishing
Maritime House
Basin Road North, Hove
BN41 1WR

Published in Australia
Crabtree Publishing
3 Charles Street
Coburg North
VIC 3058

Contents

Starting a Business 4

Career One: Pet Store Owner 6

Think Like a Pet Store Owner ·········· 7

Math Toolbox: Finding the Best Deal ····· 13

Career Pathways: Pet Store Owner······· 14

Career Two: Bakery Owner············· 15

Think Like a Future Baker ············· 16

Math Toolbox: Student Wage ·········· 20

Career Pathways: Bakery Owner ········ 21

Career Three: Video Game Designer ···· 22

Think Like a Video Game Designer ······ 23

Math Toolbox: Fractions ··············· 28

Career Pathways: Video Game Designer·· 29

Learning More & Career 1 Answers ····· 30

Glossary & Careers 1 & 2 Answers ······ 31

Index, Author's Bio, & Careers 2 & 3
       Answers 32

Please note: The standard and metric systems are used interchangeably throughout this book.

Starting a Business

Creating your own business is an opportunity to use your own gifts and abilities to make a living doing what you enjoy. Entrepeneurs **are people who start up and manage their own businesses. They are often excited and enthusiastic about their businesses and look forward to going to work each day. Imagine if you built your very own business one day!**

Every new business starts out with an idea.

Entrepreneurs start with an idea about a product or service that people would be willing to pay for. Then, they create business plans to organize how their business will run and outline what they need to do to be successful. During this planning stage, entrepreneurs use math skills to **estimate** how much it will cost to start up and run their businesses, and how much to charge for their products or services. These estimations help entrepreneurs decide if their business ideas are ready to put into action.

Some entrepreneurs sell a product, and others offer a service. A service is work someone does for someone else, such as hairstyling or tutoring.

PET STORE OWNER

Pet store owners sell products such as pet food, leashes, treats, and a variety of other items that pet owners need. Some pet stores also sell dogs, cats, birds, fish, and other pets. They may also offer services such as grooming or animal training. Pet store owners and their workers need to be very knowledgeable about the health needs of different kinds of pets.

A pet groomer helps care for cats and dogs by making sure the animals are clean and their fur and nails are trimmed.

Pet groomers can also be entrepreneurs by running their own pet care business. Sometimes they rent space in pet stores. This can help boost their business because pet owners who come into the store to buy pet supplies will find out that they can get their pet groomed there, too. This also helps the pet store owner because customers coming in to get their pets groomed might also buy supplies from the pet store owner.

Think Like a Pet Store Owner

Pet store owners must always think of ways to make their store attractive to pet owners, or people buying gifts for pet owners.

One of the most important things to know about customers is that they appreciate good service. Often, pet store owners hire **employees** to work in their stores. For the business to be successful, the employees must provide customers with good service. This means they must be friendly and knowledgeable. Employees may also take care of the pets in the store and keep the store clean. A great employee is very valuable. Store owners must decide how much to pay their employees.

1 Imagine you are a pet store owner. Weekends are the busiest days at the pet store. You need to hire a student to work on Saturdays. You pay the student $9.25 per hour. How much does the student earn for a 3-hour **shift**?

2 One of the student's jobs is to put prices on the items the store sells. Suppose you decide to give a 50-percent discount on certain items. Fill in the missing prices in the table below. (Hint: 50% is half the regular price.)

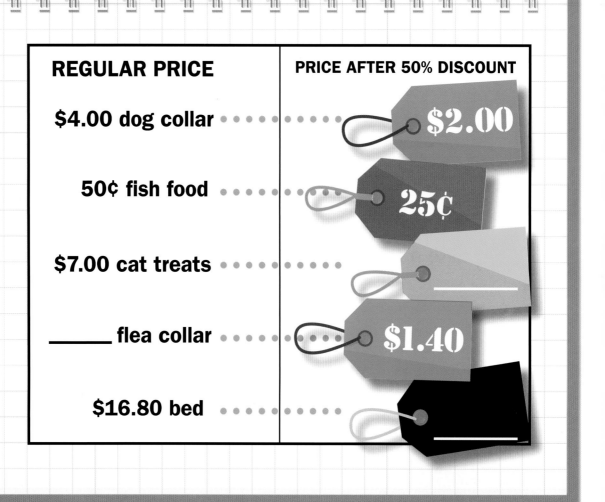

REGULAR PRICE	PRICE AFTER 50% DISCOUNT
$4.00 dog collar	$2.00
50¢ fish food	25¢
$7.00 cat treats	_____
_____ flea collar	$1.40
$16.80 bed	_____

The way a store makes money is to buy products from a supplier at a low price and then sell them to customers at a higher price. The difference between the two prices is called profit.

For example, suppose a dog food supplier sells cans of dog food to your store for 50 cents each. You sell them for 75 cents. That means that you make a profit of: 75 cents - 50 cents = 25 cents per can.

One way of calculating the price you should charge for an item is to multiply the price you paid by 100 plus the percentage you would like to make in profit. For example, if you want to make a 20% profit on every item, multiply the cost of what you paid the supplier by 100% + 20% = 120%. So, a can of cat food that cost you $1.50 would sell in your store for $1.50 X 120% = $1.80. Your profit would be 30¢ a can.

ANALYZE: Look at the table below. Do you see a pattern in the price you charge and the profit of the first two items for each dollar you spent? Use the same pattern to complete the table.

ITEM	PRICE CHARGED BY STORE	COST OF ITEM FROM SUPPLIER	PROFIT MADE BY STORE PER ITEM
Fish food	$1.50	$1.00	50¢
Dog chews	$3.00	$2.00	$1.00
Cat food	_____	$3.00	_____
Puppy bed	_____	$50.00	_____
Aquarium	_____	$200.00	_____

CALCULATE:

You decide to have a sale on certain products that have not sold well. You decide to price the products at ½ price, which is a 50% discount.

Complete the table below to find out how much to charge.

ITEM	REGULAR PRICE	SALE PRICE
aquarium	$150.00	$75.00
cat toys	$3.00	_____
bird cage	$42.50	_____
kitty litter	$7.00	_____
dog food bowl	$5.80	_____

NAMES: Josh and Holly Allen
POSITION: Pet Store Owners
BUSINESS NAME: Dee-O-Gee

How do you use math in your career?

We use math every day in many different ways. For example, we use math to calculate our product prices based on our product costs. Math is also required to find out how much food a dog should receive based on its size. We also use math to calculate payroll expenses to pay employees for the hours they work.

How has your previous math education helped you succeed in your career?

As business owners, we took math courses all the way through college, including graduate school. We wouldn't have been able to succeed at day-to-day business operations without a solid foundation in math in elementary school.

TOUGH DECISION:

You provide pet grooming services at your store. You want to offer a deal to encourage people to come in and have their pets groomed. You have come up with two different deal options and you want to figure out which of these two options will make the most money for your store:

A You offer a card that rewards the customer with one free pet grooming after four grooming visits. You decide to charge $40.00 for each grooming.

How much money will your store earn from one customer in each option? Which option makes the most money for your store? Explain how you know.

B The second option is to offer customers a special price when they purchase a package of five grooming visits. You offer five grooming visits for $175.00.

Another tough decision for a pet store owner is to decide what live animals should be sold in their store. For example, some pet store owners don't carry puppies or kittens in their stores because they want to encourage their customers to adopt a rescued pet from an animal shelter.

MATH TOOLBOX

FINDING THE BEST DEAL

You want to find which deal makes the most profit for your store.

Deal #1: Charging $2.50 for two cans of Rover Dog Food.

Deal #2: Charging $11.00 for 10 cans of Rover Dog Food.

To figure out the best deal for the store you need to find the cost of one can of dog food in each deal.

Deal #1: To find the cost of one can, divide $2.50 by 2 cans, which equals $1.25. So, selling 1 can earns the store $1.25.

Deal #2: To find the cost of 1 can, divide $11.00 by 10 cans, which equals $1.10. So, each can earns the store $1.10.

Deal #1 is best because it earns more money per can.

WANT TO BE A PET STORE OWNER?

1. Stay in school! A great education with a focus on math and science is a great beginning. College courses, such as biology and business, can help you build the knowledge and skills you will need.

2. Visit your school guidance counselor or check out your local library to find information and resources about owning a small business.

3. When you are older, consider applying for a job at a pet store to learn firsthand what it's like to work in this environment.

CAREER PATHWAYS

This could be you!

CAREER 2

BAKERY OWNER

Bakery owners are entrepreneurs who combine baking skills with business knowledge. From cakes and cookies to breads and buns, bakery owners prepare delicious baked goods for customers to enjoy. Many bakery owners are professional **bakers. They go to school to learn how to make different baked goods and how to operate special machinery used in their profession such as dough makers. Math knowledge is a key ingredient in becoming a professional baker and bakery owner.**

Imagine your dad makes the most delicious brownies you have ever tasted! They are nutty, chocolate creations that taste like a birthday party in your mouth! Your dad teaches you how to make the brownies, and you share some with your friends. Your friends love them and encourage you to sell your amazing treats. You like the idea of a brownie business! You wonder if you could sell your brownies to the corner store down the street.

Think Like a Future Baker!

You take a plate of brownies to the corner store for the owner to taste. She loves them! You suggest that you could make brownies for her store and she agrees.

These are the ingredients to make one dozen, or 12, brownies:

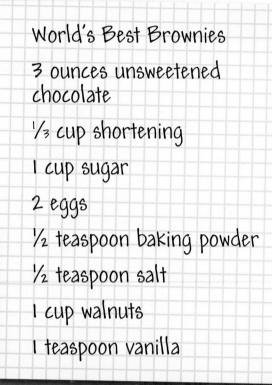

World's Best Brownies

3 ounces unsweetened chocolate

1/3 cup shortening

1 cup sugar

2 eggs

1/2 teaspoon baking powder

1/2 teaspoon salt

1 cup walnuts

1 teaspoon vanilla

1 The store owner suggests starting with an order of two dozen brownies each week. How many brownies are in two dozen?

2 How much shortening and baking powder are needed for two dozen brownies?

BAKING POWDER

Gluten Free

Net wt. 8oz 225gr

FACTS:

You have a list of ingredients for a dozen brownies. You need to calculate the cost of the ingredients so you can figure out how much you need to charge for the brownies to make a profit. Your dad agrees to supply the eggs, baking powder, salt, and vanilla. How can you calculate the cost of the other ingredients? If you go to the store, you can find the price of each ingredient. Dividing the price by the amount in the package gives you the cost of the ingredient per ounce or cup.

INGREDIENT	AMOUNT NEEDED FOR 1 DOZEN	COST TO BUY FROM STORE	COST OF INGREDIENTS FOR 1 DOZEN
unsweetened chocolate	3 ounces	$1.63 per ounce	_____
shortening	1/3 cup	66¢ per cup	_____
sugar	1 cup	30¢ per cup	_____
walnuts	1 cup	$1.19 per cup	_____
Total cost for 1 dozen brownies			_____

ANALYZE:

1 a) In the table above, calculate the cost of each ingredient needed to make a dozen brownies.

b) What is the total cost to make one dozen brownies?

c) Based on the total cost, find the cost of the ingredients needed to make just one brownie. This is the minimum price you must charge per brownie to cover your costs.

2 One way a business owner might figure out how to make a profit is to set a product's price at three times the amount the product costs to make. What is the price of one brownie if you charge three times the amount it costs you to make it?

3 Many prices end with the number zero. If the price for a brownie does not end with a zero, you can round it up to the nearest 10 cents. If you calculated a price of 46 cents, for example, you could round it to 50 cents per brownie.

a) How much money would you make from selling two dozen brownies at the rounded price for each one?

b) What is your profit after you subtract the cost of the ingredients?

TOUGH DECISION:

You get a call from the store owner and she wants to sell your brownies in her store. She wants two dozen brownies every day. Before you agree to this, you want to do some calculations and see whether it is worth your time.

1 It takes you 2 hours to make and deliver two dozen brownies. Using the profit you calculated and the time it takes to make the brownies, find out how much you would earn per hour.

2 How much would your profit be if you baked and delivered 2 dozen brownies each day for seven days?

MATH
TOOLBOX

STUDENT WAGE

1. How much would a student who is paid $10.50 per hour earn if they worked 7 hours in one week?

2. How does the hourly amount in the example above compare to the hourly amount of money earned from selling two dozen brownies a day?

3. What might be one negative thing about a student working every day, especially on school nights?

This could be you!

WANT TO BE A BAKERY OWNER?

1. Stay in school! A great education with a focus on cooking and math is the key. There are culinary arts schools that help you increase your knowledge of baking. Practice baking recipes at home. Let your family and friends be your taste-testers.

2. Visit your school guidance counselor or local library and ask about colleges and technical schools that offer culinary arts programs that will help you become a pastry chef.

3. Contact a local baker and ask if you could meet them in person to ask questions. Find out what kinds of math they must do in their job.

CAREER PATHWAYS

CAREER 3

VIDEO GAME DESIGNER

A video game designer creates the story line, scenes, and characters that make video games amazing experiences. To work in video game design, an understanding of computers and mathematics is important. Future designers can go to schools that offer programs in the art and science of video game design.

Think Like a Video Game Designer

Imagine you want to create an around-the-world race game. The characters in the game must travel the world and compete in contests as they go. Your job is to create contests to be played along the way. You decide each contest win is worth 1,000 points, and each **destination** arrived at is worth 2,000 points. It costs points to travel to each new destination. The character who collects the most points at the end of the game wins.

SOLVE:

The first contest you create is to have players estimate the number of gumballs in a container. You buy a package of gumballs and count them. You count 136 gumballs and use this number in the game.

1 Player 1 estimates there are 121 gumballs. What is the difference between their guess and the actual number of gumballs?

2 Player 2 guessed twice as many gumballs as there actually are. How many gumballs did they guess?

3 Player 3 was off by 31 gumballs. How many did they guess? Why are there two possible answers?

4 The player with the estimation closest to the actual amount wins. You review each player's estimation. Which player wins the contest?

ANALYZE:

The players must pay for their travel with points they earn from the contests. One of the contestants has earned 1,000 points.

1 Suppose the travel expenses for the trip include:
- a flight which costs 750 points
- the subway which costs 50 points
- a taxi which costs 22 points

Does the player with 1,000 points have enough to make the trip?

2 Suppose there are eight flights for each player to make. The distance of each flight is a fraction of the trip's whole distance. You decide to test the players' abilities to put fractions in order. You choose four flights from the trip and ask the players to put the fractions in order from smallest to greatest.

The parts of the trip given as fractions are: $\frac{1}{4}$, $\frac{1}{5}$, $\frac{1}{3}$, and $\frac{1}{6}$

a) Put the fractions in order from smallest to greatest.

b) How much greater is $\frac{1}{3}$ than $\frac{1}{6}$? Describe how you know.

DECIDE:

As the video game designer, you decide that another challenge in the game will be based on the players' travel time. Players must find which flight will get them to their destination in the shortest amount of time. **Rank** the flights from 1 to 4, with 1 being the shortest flight and 4 being the longest flight. Players that correctly rank the flights win 1,000 points each.

Complete the table below:

FLIGHT START TIME	FLIGHT END TIME	TOTAL FLIGHT TIME	RANK
11:00 a.m.	2:00 p.m.	_____	_____
7:00 a.m.	9:30 a.m.	_____	_____
12:00 p.m.	1:30 p.m.	_____	_____
11:00 p.m.	1:00 a.m.	_____	_____

TOUGH DECISION:

You have to decide whether the contestants' leftover travel points can be added to the points they get for being first at a destination. You want to make the game fair. You must make some choices.

1 Suppose a player receives 2,000 points to start the game. They use 1,804 points to get to the first destination. How many points are left over?

2 If the same player wins a contest at that destination, they earn 1,000 points. How many points do they have now if they add in their leftover travel points?

3 Suppose a contestant saves enough points to travel straight to the final destination. They choose not to compete in the remaining contests, and collect an extra 3,000 points by arriving at the final destination first. That will win them the game. If they did not compete in all the contests, do you think they deserve to win the game, or should you change the rules? Explain your opinion.

YOU WIN!

FRACTIONS

It can sometimes be a challenge to compare the sizes of fractions. Fractions with 1 as the numerator, such as in ⅓ and ⅕, can be compared by making a drawing of a circle and dividing up the circle to represent the number in the denominator.

For example, ⅓ looks like this:

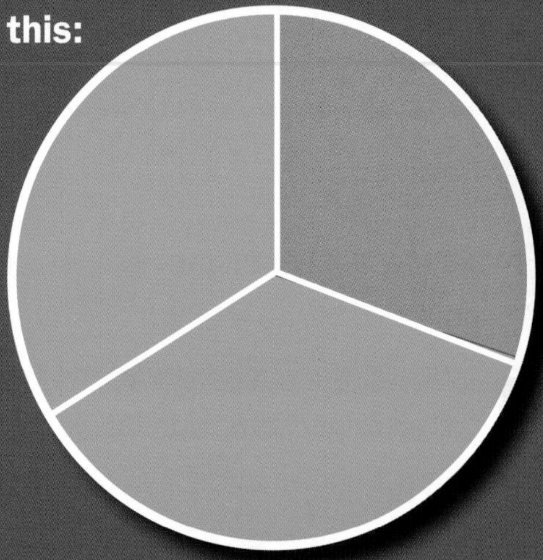

⅕ looks like this:

Look at the size of the red piece in each circle. It is clear that ⅓ is greater than ⅕ because ⅓ is a larger piece of the circle.

WANT TO BE A VIDEO GAME DESIGNER?

1. Stay in school! A great education with lots of science and math is the key. Consider going to a school that offers courses in animation in a digital environment.

2. Visit your school guidance counselor or local library and ask about colleges that offer digital art courses.

3. The site below gives an inside look at how video game designers use math. Check it out!

www.thirteen.org/get-the-math/the-challenges/math-in-videogames/introduction/16/

CAREER PATHWAYS

This could be you!

Websites

In this game, players run their own coffee shop and practice business math skills by purchasing supplies and calculating profits:
www.coolmath-games.com/0-coffee-shop

Developed by Warren Buffet, this website focuses on entrepreneurial skills for kids. Content includes webisodes from the Secret Millionaire's Club, math games, and interactive quizzes:
www.smckids.com/games.php

This site gives terrific information about the qualities of a successful video game designer:
http://electronics.howstuffworks.com/video-game-designer.htm

Books

Arroyo, Sheri, L. *How Chefs Use Math*. Chelsea House, 2010.

Egan, Jill. *How Video Game Designers Use Math*. Chelsea House, 2010.

Minden, Cecilia. *Starting Your Own Business*: Real World Math. Cherry Lake Publishing, 2016.

Shafer, Sonya. *Pet Store* (Student Kit). Your Business Math Series: Simply Charlotte Mason.

ANSWERS

Career 1: Pet Store Owner

Solve: 1) 3 hrs x $9.25 = $27.75. The student would earn $27.75.

2) Cat treats = $7 x 50% = $3.50, Flea collars = $1.40 x 2 = $2.80,
   Bed = $16.80 x 50% = $8.40

Analyze: The pattern is for every $1.00 you spend, you
charge $1.50 and make a 50¢ profit.

cat food price = $3.00 x $1.50 = $4.50

cat food profit = $3.00 x $0.50 = $1.50

puppy bed price = $50.00 x $1.50 = $75.00

puppy bed profit = $50.00 x $0.50 = $25.00

aquarium price = $200.00 x $1.50 = $300.00

aquarium profit = $200.00 x $0.50 = $100.00

Calculate:

aquarium = $150.00 x ½ = $75.00

cat toys = $3.00 x ½ = $1.50

bird cage = $42.50 x ½ = $21.25

kitty litter = $7.00 x ½ = $3.50

dog food bowl = $5.80 x ½ = $2.90

Glossary

animation To use drawings or models to create the illusion of movement

biology Having to do with living things

culinary To do with cooking

deominator In a fraction, the number below the line

destination The ending place of a journey

digital Referring to electronic technology

employee Someone who works for money

entrepeneur A person who runs a business that involves significant risk and initiative

estimate To make an approximate calculation or guess

numerator In a fraction, the number above the line

professional A person who gets paid for their skills

rank To place in order

profit The amount left after the costs have been subtracted from the price

shift An amount of time that a worker is required to be on duty

supplier A company or area that produces raw materials or parts of a product

ANSWERS CONTINUED

Career 1: Pet Store Owner

Tough Decision: Using option A, a customer would pay 4x$40 = $160.00 for five grooming visits. Using option B, a customer would pay $175.00 for five grooming visits. Therefore, option B earns more money for your business for the same number of groomings.

Career 2: Bakery Owner

Solve: 1) 2 x 12 = 24 brownies 2) 2 x 1/3 = 2/3 cup of shortening, 2 x 1/2 = 1 teaspoon baking powder

Analyze: 1. a) unsweetened chocolate = 3 x $1.63 = $4.89, shortening = 1/3 x $0.66 = $0.22, sugar = 1 x $0.30 = $0.30, walnuts = 1 x $1.19 = $1.19

   b) $4.89 + $0.22 + $0.30 + $1.19 = $6.60. The total cost for 1 dozen brownies is $6.60.

   c) $6.60/12 = $0.55. The minimum price you must charge is 55¢ per brownie.

   2. $0.55 x 3 = $1.65

   3. a) $1.70 x 24 brownies = $40.80

   b) Cost for 2 dozen brownies = $6.60 x 2 = $13.20. Profit = $40.80-$13.20 = $27.60

Tough Decision: 1) $27.60/2 hours = $13.80 per hour

   2) $27.60 x 7 = $193.20 profit after seven days

Index

cost 5, 9, 10, 11, 13, 16, 18, 23, 25
denominator 28
difference/subtract 9, 18, 24
divide 13, 17, 28
earnings 19, 20, 25
estimate 5, 24
fractions 25, 28
multiply 9
numerator 28
percent 8, 9, 11
pricing 8, 9, 10, 11, 12, 17, 18
profit 9, 10, 13, 17, 18, 19
rounding 18, 19
time 19, 26

ANSWERS CONTINUED

Career 2: Bakery Owner:

Math Toolbox: Student wage: 1) $10.50 x 7 = $73.50 for 7 hours a week
2) The hourly wage for making brownies is $13.80. That is $3.30 more an hour.
3) They might be more tired and find it harder to concentrate on their schoolwork.

Career 3: Video Game Designer

Solve: 1) 136-121 = 15 gumballs to few, 2) 2 x 136 = 272 gumballs, 3) 136-31 = 105, or 136 + 31 = 167. They could have been over or under. 4) Player 1 wins. They were the closest.

Analyze: 1. Yes, they have enough points. They have used only 822 of their 1,000 points
2. a) $\frac{1}{6}$, $\frac{1}{5}$, $\frac{1}{4}$, $\frac{1}{3}$ b) $\frac{1}{3} = \frac{2}{6}$, so $\frac{1}{3}$ is two times greater than $\frac{1}{6}$.

Decide:

Flight start time	Flight end time	Total flight time	Rank
11:00 a.m.	2:00 p.m.	3 hours	4
7:00 a.m.	9:30 a.m.	2.5 hours	3
12:00 p.m.	1:30 p.m.	1.5 hours	1
11:00 p.m.	1:00 a.m.	2 hours	2

Tough Decision:
1) 2,000 - 1804 = 196 points
2) 196 + 1,000 = 1,196
3) Answers may vary.

Author Bio:

Rick loves pets, brownies, and even video games. He also loves being an entrepreneur by creating math books, science books, and young reader novels for schools. Rick enjoys learning about science and math and has the best job in the world for him—a teacher.